YES YOU CAN!
10 Great Ways to Market Your Business

By: Cynthia McCalister, MS

Copyright © 2018 Cynthia McCalister

All rights reserved.

ISBN-13: 978-1984095398
ISB-10: 1984095390

DEDICATION

In memory of my parents Thomas and Madlyn Johnson. Forever in my heart. Their influence and inspiration lives on.

CONTENTS

	Acknowledgments	i
1	Introduction	Pg 1
2	Did You Hear Me on the Radio	Pg 3
3	Making Social Media Work for You & Your Brand	Pg 13
4	Having a Mobile Mindset	Pg 32
5	Paper Please	Pg 40
6	Lights, Camera, Action	Pg 49
7	No Work Without Network	Pg 54
8	Send it Now	Pg 63
9	Put it in Writing	Pg 73
10	Presented by You	Pg 79
11	Franchise You	Pg 89
12	Make Lemons into Lemonade	Pg 94
13	Motivating Mavens	Pg 98
14	Words of Wisdom	Pg 106
15	Closing	Pg 118
	About the Author	Pg 121
	Want to Learn More	Pg 123
	Notes	Pg 124

ACKNOWLEDGMENTS

To my Husband Daniel for his ongoing love and support.

My wonderful children LaDawn and DJ for listening to me whenever I had something exciting to share, participating in my vision, and believing in my dream.

My sister Shannetta for constantly being a source of knowledge, support, and uplifting light. Always telling me to document my journey, because one day I can share my story and help inspire others. I'm glad I listened to her.

My sister Michelle for reminding me how proud she is of me, and how proud our parents would be too. Those special words of support helped to motivate and keep me going.

1 INTRODUCTION

Being a small business owner is not always an easy thing. You will hear many, "no's", and cash doesn't always flow the way you want it to. Sometimes, the hardest part is getting people to know about you as a business, and putting your name into the atmosphere. According to the Spark Business Barometer survey conducted by Capital One, "Seventy-Six percent of small business owners, report facing marketing challenges." As a small business owner, I have marketed my business in many ways, from going door-to-door, cold calling and by using social media to share my business.

By taking many different approaches, I have finally unlocked the door to effective business marketing! Now, I have a business where users throughout the country are utilizing the Key Spot mobile app, which was created by my company, Quality SAP. And, guess what? You can do it too! You can get people to know your brand. Don't think you're too out of touch to get your brand out there, or think it's too expensive or complicated to figure out. In my book, I will give you ten ways to successfully market your business.

Now it's your turn to apply the lessons I have learned and use them for yourself! I want to share with you, what I have found to be successful for marketing my products and services, as well as affordable tools and practices to get you on the way to successfully market your business. With the information you gain from my book, you will be able to apply the learnings that I share to your own business, and in the long run, improve your marketing success.

2 RADIO: *DID YOU HEAR ME ON THE RADIO*

"Ambition is the path to success. Persistence is the vehicle you arrive in."

Bill Bradley

What comes to mind when you think of radio? Do you imagine an old outdated form of media, or maybe the talk radio morning show on your commute to work? More people listen to radio on a daily basis than you might think, "90 percent of commuters listen to traditional AM/FM radio, while in their car." (Edison Research, 2016). In addition to traditional radio, online and satellite radio are becoming more popular. "Online radio is playing an increasing role in the radio market, with an estimated 61 percent of the US population listening to online radio in 2017." (Statista.com, 2017). In addition, "News/talk radio is the number one overall format of radio." (Nielson.com, 2017). Given this data, there is more to explore when it comes to utilizing the power of radio to market your business.

The Power of Radio

There are many ways you can utilize the power of radio to market your business. One way is by creating a radio ad. Radio advertisements are effective because not only will your ad be played repeatedly throughout the course of the day, but if you purchase multiple spots, you will eventually reach your target audience.

Typically, the cost for a radio advertisement is $500 or more. You can have a radio ad about 30 seconds long play several times a day over the course of a specified timeframe, based on your marketing budget.

Some important factors when creating a radio commercial is to, know your target audience and be sure the message you want to convey is crystal clear. It's also important to have a good script and get straight to the point. Repetition is key. Adding humor and music are also good ways to make your ad more memorable. Work with the radio marketing department to get the best options to make you advertising successful. Select the best ad package for you, which will enable you to share the message you want to get across to the radio listeners.

The Benefits of a Radio Ad

According to smallbusinesschronicles.com, there are several benefits of having a radio ad for your business. The first is, "Radio is an innate form of advertising. Many people listen alone such as jogging or driving. Listeners develop strong relationships with their favorite stations, identifying with the music and bonding with on-air personalities." (Zeske, 2018). Secondly, according to Leightonbroadcasting.com, "you can put a voice with a brand", and you will most certainly be able to "connect with consumers". (Theisen, 2017).

Oftentimes, while riding with my kids in the car, a familiar radio ad with a jingle will air and they will sing along. You know, the jingles that will more-than-likely get stuck in your head? Well, that is the end-goal for any business, to be remembered. Good marketing is when you get a jingle stuck in your head to the point where you eventually end up purchasing the goods or services of the brand. Just think, you can be that brand! Be creative, and make your ad fun! Then, when you're driving down the road, and you hear your commercial, you can call your friends and say, "Hey, did you hear me on the radio?!"

Want To Do More Than Just a Radio Ad?

There are many other options you can choose if you want to do more than a radio ad to market your business. Have you ever considered a radio interview? You might think that radio interviews are only for celebrities but, that isn't always the case. Going the radio interview route gives you more time to share information about your business. Usually, a radio interview can last anywhere between ten to twenty minutes, which is enough time for you to delve deeper into what products and services your business offers.

Reach out to a Radio Station

There are several ways to be considered for having your brand presence on the radio. The first is by personally reaching out to a radio stations producer. Let the producer know what your business is all about, and why you'd want to be featured on their show.

My Experience

One morning while I was driving, I heard Jen Fritsch a radio DJ and producer of the "Jeff and Jenn Morning Show" on Q102, share her interest in wanting to use a specialized photography service. I instantly perked up, because that was exactly the service that my company offered! After I heard that, I contacted my business director Denise, and she immediately reached out to Jen Fritsch and offered her our services free of charge. Shortly thereafter, Denise received a response from Jen regarding the opportunity, and wanting to learn more. A time was scheduled to go to the radio station, introduce our company to Jen, and schedule a photography session (which by the way, Jen accepted the offer!)

After meeting and working with Jen Fritsch, she then shared her experience of working with my company with her friends and followers on social media. Not only did she share it on her radio podcast, but she also posted pictures on her Facebook page, which also created a buzz about my business!

Jen Fritsch radio DJ and producer of "Jeff & Jenn Morning Show" Q102 FM & Cynthia following Pure Silk photo shoot February 2014.

Free is Always Good

When you are trying to get your brand known, offering goods and services always peeks a potential customer's interest. There are several benefits of providing a potential customer goods and services free of charge. According to ideasforsmallbiz.com, "People who have some sort of community influence will help to "create a buzz" about your company". Secondly, it will "encourage others to try your products and or services risk-free." (ideasforsmallbiz.com).

I am grateful for my experience working with Jen Fritsch. My experience is only an example of gaining exposure and connecting with someone who is a community influencer. If this is the route you want to take with branding your business, you may discover that the people you reach out to may be willing and open to working with you. When reaching out to anyone who is a community influencer, some pieces of advice to remember is that persistence is key. Secondly, always be aware of opportunities that may come your way. Lastly, don't forget to act upon the opportunities that are offered to you, because you never know when those opportunities will be available to you again.

Talk Radio Interviews

Another way to enter the world of radio is through talk Radio. Radio stations often offer a specific scheduled time, which caters to sharing information about activities and businesses within the community. Being a guest on a talk radio show will allow you to share your business, and what you have to offer. The cost to be a guest on a radio show may be more affordable then you think. You can find radio stations that may feature you as a guest for around $200 and up, which is far less than purchasing a spot for your radio ad.

As a person who is not famous, but wanting to get on a radio talk show, you might ask, where do I start? Going the paid interview route is one great option to go. With this option, the benefits are spending less money than a radio commercial, but having more time to tell your story. Many radio stations offer scheduled time dedicated to sharing information about activities and businesses in the community. There are many AM and some FM stations that have programs targeting the community, just waiting to get you on the air. With this opportunity, you can spend a full 15 -25 minutes on air sharing your story and pitching your business at a reasonable cost.

I had a great time as a guest on a radio talk show. Thousands of listeners heard my talk radio interview throughout the day. The very thought of having so many people listening to you, tends to make some people nervous. It is important to know what you want to get across during your interview, and what you want the listeners to know about your brand. It is also important to prepare for your interview beforehand so you can be sure that every aspect of your business is mentioned.

How to Prepare For Your Radio Interview

There are several steps in order to prepare for your radio interview. According to prnews.online.com, you should "know who the primary audience is." And, you should also, "anticipate any and all questions that you will be asked." (Fitzgerald, 2016) When speaking about your brand, you should be clear about the products and services that you provide. Lastly, be sure to mention any upcoming events and your business website.

There is joy and excitement about sharing your brand. Be sure that you are not only prepared, but be relaxed and have fun! I would highly recommend having the experience of an on air interview. It is one way to spend more time promoting your cause at an affordable price. Plus, you never know who may be listening.

Pamela Pitts Host of LIFE THE L'BAE WAY radio broadcast on AM 1050 & 103.1 FM & Cynthia March 2017.

Statistics:

- Radio is an affordable way to promote your business. "Radio is the most cost effective medium for your ad dollar." (strategicmediainc.com)

- "Radio reaches more consumers." (Nielson.com)

- With a radio commercial there are multiple spots and opportunities for people to hear your pitch.

- With an on air interview you have more time to promote your cause.

- "Radio supports retention because of cognitive processing radio is so much more effective at influencing behavior. And because radio is often part of our communities and daily habits, it is trusted more." (strategicmediainc.com)

Chapter 2 Tips: Getting Your Brand's Message Across Using Radio

- When creating a radio advertisement, be creative and make it memorable.

- Be sure to add humor and music to your radio advertisement.

- During the radio interview let the audience know about the product and services your business offers.

- Look up radio stations and reach out to the producer via email to offer your services.

- When speaking with the producer, be sure to mention you are a listener and looking to share your services complimentary.

3 UTILIZING SOCIAL MEDIA: MAKING SOCIAL MEDIA WORK FOR YOU & YOUR BRAND

"The most valuable thing you can make is a mistake – you can't learn anything from being perfect."

Adam Osborne

In this chapter, we will specifically touch on Facebook, LinkedIn, Instagram, and how they can be utilized to help you market your brand. We will discuss how to effectively use them for your benefit, based on their unique platforms.

Just to note, as time progresses, some application features may change, due to the nature of technology. But, you have to start somewhere. According to Oxforddictionary.com, the definition of Social Media is, "Websites and applications that enable users to create and share content or participate in social networking." (oxforddictionary.com, 2018). Social Media is an ever growing and ever changing form of media. Facebook, Instagram, and LinkedIn are great platforms to use for promoting your brand and business. Typically, the demographics utilizing Facebook is 30+, whereas, the younger audience (18-30), prefer Instagram. Those who are industry professionals, tend to use LinkedIn as a tool for networking and connecting with other professionals.

All Social Media platforms mentioned can serve as a way to assist you with marketing your brand. Since users of Facebook are typically older than those who use Instagram, you want to be sure to cater to the specific audience you are attempting to reach. For instance, when marketing your brand to Instagram users, imagery is everything and the less wording you have, the better. Being bold and catching the attention of those within your target market is key.

FACEBOOK

Soon after I joined Facebook, I started to create a page for my business. Having a page for your business is a great way to share information about your company. It also gives you the opportunity to share your page with your friends and with groups that you may be a member of. It gives you the ability to include any events and announcements that your business might have.

Creating a page for your business is almost like building a website. In addition, you can draw in an audience, by creating interactive content, photos, videos, and organizing contests. Sharing daily and weekly content will help you to engage viewers and build followers. When you ask others to "Like" your Facebook page, that increases your statistics of outreach as well as viewership.

Facebook is one of the largest social media networks. It has been around since February 2004. Everyday new users join, and people enjoy it because they have the ability to share and receive information, no matter if it's from friends, relatives, the community or news. Facebook is also a great place for business owners to share and promote their brand, utilizing features available. Some examples include the publish tools and instant articles. To expand your audience, Facebook allows you to promote your posts at a cost starting around $5. According to Google.com, "Page posts only reach about 16% of a company's fan base, so businesses often pay to have their status updates appear in people's news feed. These can only be targeted to fans and friends of fans. The cost varies on how many fans you want to target, but costs about $5 for every 1,000 people you want to target." (Google.com, 2013)

Leveraging Facebook Ads

Facebook advertising can help you reach new audiences in an effective manner. You will also have the ability to track clicks, reach, and impressions for metrics. The data available from the advertising is quite helpful, allowing you to know what information people are interested in, what works, and what doesn't work.

When you have a Facebook page for your business, you may routinely receive notifications from Facebook, offering to share your pictures and video content as Facebook advertising. Having your content shared via Facebook advertising is a great option. Be sure your message is succinct, making it consumable for a wider audience who may not be familiar with your brand. If you choose to utilize the paid advertising, be sure you have a brief and clear marketing ad that will get your message across to help you obtain followers.

Establishing Facebook Groups

As I built my following on Facebook, I initially began by joining groups and connecting with other business owners to grow my network. After not receiving the speed in growth that I was looking for, I re-evaluated my situation and changed direction to take a different approach. That's when I decided to create the Key Spot Business Partners' Facebook group and began publishing my own content. This group was created as a way to celebrate and support small businesses, artists, and musicians in order for them to share what they were doing in the community. Today, I have thousands of business owners from across the country that are part of the Key Spot Network, spreading and supporting positivity and awareness about the Key Spot app.

> *"Key Spot Business Partners is a great community to build business partnerships and to promote your business."* **- Darrin Brown, Founder of Dynamic Leadership Empowerment Group (Houston, TX)**

> *"Thank you for supporting our brand we truly appreciate you."* **- Shakira Johnson, Owner of Kira's Kouture Boutique (Baltimore, MD)**

> *"Thank you! It means so much to have this support."* **- Karen Burno-Wallace, Owner of Meta Naturals (Cincinnati, OH)**

> *"Thank you for the smile and thoughts and your time for all you do for giving me your support."* **- Angie Clay, Owner of Designation Concierge (Detroit, MI)**

"Thank you!! You really help keep me going!" - Nalia Smoot, Owner of Essential Oasis Massage (Cincinnati, OH)

"So thankful for Key Spot. Blessings to the companies featured on this platform." - Louise Ellison, Program Director of Face 2 Face Radio Talk Show on KLAY AM 1180 (Lakewood, WA)

"I am so excited about the Key Spot app! This amazing app connects small business owners, influencers, authors, and speakers in a mobile directory based on location." - Whitney Barkley, Owner of Speakerazzi (Columbus, OH)

"Your company has been so amazaing this year helping us to prmotoe our brand. We greatly appreciate it!" - Rosemary Oglesby-Henry, CEO of Roseemary's Babies Co. (Cincinnati, OH)

"Any business looking for ad promotion and networking check out Key Spot Face Book Page and Key Spot App." **- Leatriece G. Franklin, Owner of LF Mobile Lifesaving Courses (Memphis, TN)**

"Our business listing is available on Key Spot. The app is quite useful!" **- Earnest Alexander, Owner of Fast Signs (Carrollwood, Tampa, FL)**

Steps to Building a Following

When it comes to building a following on social media, content is key. My goal was to increase my group membership and keep those who were already members, interested. The three keys that I found to keep Facebook members interested in continuing to take part were Interaction, Support, and Celebration

Interaction:

Be sure you reach out to the community and ask questions. Get people engaged in discussion. Organize creative contests to encourage users to participate.

Show Support

Showcase businesses who are followers, and share the positive things they are doing in the community. Recognize them by their business name, and encourage their events and the activities they organize.

I try to attend and participate in member events, whenever possible and include congratulatory messages. Most importantly, members enjoy having someone give them encouragement and support on a routine basis. Also, at the end of each week, we publish celebration posts and shout out businesses and achievers by name, for taking action and making things happen

Communicate Your Purpose

In order for your Facebook group to work, it is important to identify your purpose. Find what the key ingredients are for your group that helps to make it work and grow. This, in turn, will help you market your brand and bring exposure to your business and social media landscape. At the top of your group, pin a clear statement of the purpose for your group, allowing visitors to determine if this is the right group for them and members to know what to expect as they participate and interact with others.

YES YOU CAN! 10 GREAT WAYS TO MARKET YOUR BUSINESS

Stevie Swain (Owner of CinCWN), Cynthia, & Donise Coleman (Owner of Royal Creations), January 2018.

The big thing that keeps people posting and part of the group is knowing there is someone on their side encouraging and supporting them each week. It is challenging having your own business. Statistics state 80% of businesses fail within 18 months, (Forbes.com). We demonstrate our support each week by publishing a celebration post to call out by name the businesses and achievers taking action to make things happen.

For your group, identify what your purpose is and find the key ingredients to make it work and grow. In turn this will help you market your brand and get your name expanded throughout the social media landscape.

Facebook Live

Facebook Live has become a popular feature on Facebook. It's a great tool for you to share your businesses' activities and events with your followers in real time. It's almost as if you have your own show! According to sproutsocial.com, Facebook Live is an effective marketing tool for your brand because it, "allows you to better connect with your audience," and it "increases awareness around community events." (York, 2017). In order for your Facebook Live videos to be effective, consider designating specific dates, times and events when the feature is used. For instance, you can host a live stream once a week, for 20 minutes. Be sure to cover topics that will capture the interest of your followers, so they will remain tuned in and want to hear what you have to share.

A helpful suggestion for your Facebook Live content, is to consider having your content transcribed to include subtitles. After the transcription is complete, you can upload it onto the Facebook platform and add the subtitles to your live stream. Doing so will allow your viewers to watch your live stream, without sound or, it can also be for those who are hearing impaired who may want to view your content.

LINKEDIN

If you are a professional, and you're looking to network and grow your presence with other professionals, LinkedIn is the best platform for you. This platform comes highly recommended as one of the most effective tools for professional networking. LinkedIn, is targeted more for the business-to-business audience and is a hub for not only professionals, but also individuals, organizations, and companies to come together and to share information such as job opportunities, articles, news, and resume information.

Build Connections Utilizing LinkedIn

As a business owner, I am always looking to connect and network with other industry professionals. LinkedIn, is a great tool to help you expand your network. It allows you to connect with people who are business owners, or influencers who can connect you to others who may be interested in your product or service.

My Experience

One day, on my Key Spot Business Partner Facebook page, one of the members shared an event that supported women business owners and those interested in starting their own business. I saw the post and immediately wanted to learn more about the event. The organizer of the event was not part of the group, but her name was provided in the event post. I then decided I wanted to connect with her. Given the professional nature of LinkedIn, I started there searching for her profile. I logged into my LinkedIn account and did a search, which successfully lead me to the right person. I sent her a communication via LinkedIn messenger, and shortly thereafter, she responded. I eventually became a sponsor for the event titled, "She Was Made Summit" and the organizer of the event, Gail Lee Gardner, became a Key Spot Growth Partner, which helps to support and spread the word about the Key Spot App.

Ways to Connect On LinkedIn:

- Join groups
- Send custom-made requests to those you want to connect with

Once you establish specific connections, be sure to check out their connections to build your own network. Use the tool wisely and you never know where the connections may take you.

Cynthia & Gail Lee Gardner, owner of "She Was Made LLC" at "She Was Made Summit" October 2017.

Creating Articles and Sharing Posts via LinkedIn

A feature that I have found to be beneficial for marketing my business, is the article functionality. When you publish articles, it gives your brand more exposure. When you allow your settings to be accessible to the public, industry professionals and influencers can read your articles.

When branding my business, I try to publish an average of one to two articles per week. I focus on key topics such as a detailed spotlight of business owners making a difference in the community or weekly shout outs to multiple businesses, showing support for what they do.

To come up with ideas to write about, find what your brand's niche is and share content on a routine basis. A suggestion would be, make sure you share your published articles on multiple social media platforms. Don't forget to tag people on the posts that are sent out, so their followers can see it as well. When it comes to searches and putting your brand on the map, a suggestion would be to utilize hashtags within your published articles. The hashtags will help increase your popularity. Keep the same hashtags each time so the posts can accumulate under the same umbrella.

INSTAGRAM

Of all the social media platforms mentioned, Instagram is the most visual. Utilize this platform for eye-catching pictures and videos in order to get the attention and interest of followers. According to stastista.com, Instagram users are between the ages of 18-34. That's 16% females and 18% males, between the ages of 18-24; 15% females and 15% males, between the ages of 25-34. (statista.com).

If you choose to use Instagram to market your brand, it's important to share videos that are amusing and photos that are visually appealing to get the most attention. So, be sure to use Instagram wisely and post frequently.

Engaging Followers on Instagram

Engagement on Instagram with your followers is very important. Some ways you could do that is by, creating an exciting challenge, or contest, where prizes or giveaways are involved. Once again, use hashtags to help make your marketing campaign trend. If posting a picture is a requirement for your contest, ask the participants to also include the hashtags on their pictures. The hashtags will help increase your popularity, and referencing your name in shared photos will also open your brand to a wider audience

Statistics

- With over 467 million members worldwide, LinkedIn is one of the most popular social networks in terms of active users. **(Statista)**

- Facebook is used by 79% percent of internet users **(Statista)**

- Instagram is used by 32% of internet users **(Statista)**

- LinkedIn is used by 29% of internet users **(Statista)**

- 13% of Millennial (15-34 Years old) use LinkedIn. **(omnicoreagency)**

- 44% of Linked users earn more than $75,000 in a year. **(omnicoreagency)**

- There are 57% of male users and 44% female users on LinkedIn. **(LinkedIn)**

- Engagement rates on Instagram are 15 times higher than Facebook and 20 higher than Twitter. 73% of brands post at least one photo or video per week on Instagram. **(simplymearured)**

- Visual data is processed 60K times faster by the brain than text. **(Business2community)**

- 40% of people will respond better to visual information than plain text. **(oursocialtimes)**

- 65% of your audience are visual learners. **(Business2community)**

- On Facebook, photos perform best for likes, comments, and shares as compared to text, video, and links. **(danzarrella)**

- Social Media Content (other than blogs) is the #1 B2B Content Marketing Tactic Usage among businesses. 93% of the organizations use social media content, 82% use Case Studies, 81% use Blogs and 81% use e-newsletters, too. **(Content Marketing Institute)**

- 94% organizations use LinkedIn for content distribution; 87% use Twitter, 84% use Facebook, while 74% use YouTube. **(Content Marketing Institute)**

- As far as B2C content marketing tactics are concerned, 90% use Social Media Content (other than blogs), 87% Photos/Illustrations, 83% use e-newsletters, while Videos, Articles on Website and Blogs get 82%, 81%, and 77% score, respectively. **(Content Marketing Institute)**

- Among social media platforms for B2C content marketing, 94% rely on Facebook, 82% use Twitter, 77% utilize YouTube and 76% also use LinkedIn. **(Content Marketing Institute)**

Chapter 3 Tips: Ways to Utilize Social Media for Marketing

- Facebook
    - Create a Facebook page for your business/brand
    - Establish your own Facebook group, specific to your business, brand, service or event
    - Build your following using friends from your personal page and from other groups

- Post content that will engage your followers
- Take advantage of Facebook Ads
- Try Facebook Live and share on a routine basis

- LinkedIn
    - Use LinkedIn to help build your business network
    - Build connections and reach out to people in order to build new relationships
    - Share posts on a routine basis
    - Write compelling articles

- Instagram
    - Know your audience
    - Post frequently
    - Consistently comment on industry influencers Instagram page and ask them to mention you in their posts
    - Share your Instagram page

- - Share eye-catching photos and videos in order to get the attention of new followers
  - Utilize contests and giveaways to boost engagement

- Suggestions for Utilizing Social Media

  - Post routinely on Facebook, LinkedIn, and Instagram.
  - For each post on social media, utilize hashtags that are commonly used.
  - Reference other posts that use hashtags, to get ideas.
  - Don't be afraid to send a message to an industry influencer on social media.
  - Leverage the statistics metrics and data tools available in each platform.

4 KEY SPOT MOBILE APP MARKETING: HAVING A MOBILE MINDSET

"Do. Or do not. There is no try."
Yoda

In 2015 McDonalds and Burger King launched their own mobile apps, providing customers the opportunity to get deals and discounts on their products. These multi-billion dollar companies can easily build out the app of their dreams. Many companies look to create their own mobile apps to draw customers and share their information, however due to the high cost of mobile app development and marketing, it is not feasible for small business owners. The cost can be in the tens or hundreds or thousands of dollars.

There are other platforms that businesses have looked to in order to take advantage of the marketing, sales, and coupon functionality available such as Groupon or Reach Magazine. But, there is only one that offers mobile marketing using coupons along with being a community centered platform sharing events, services, and business information all in one, **Key Spot**.

The idea for the Key Spot Mobile App came to me in a dream in April 2015. When I woke up, the first thing I did was grab a notepad and a pen and wrote it down. My idea was to develop a platform that people could use for business and in the community. The Key Spot Mobile App was designed to help users find and post things such as restaurant deals, business information, school events, garage sales, festivals and concerts all in one place.

I eventually shared my concept with my sister, Shannetta. She liked my concept, but asked questions such as, "What made my idea different from my competitors?" which was a thought I contemplated. I wanted to clearly articulate the importance of developing my platform. It's always a good idea to know what your niche is and what's special about what you have to offer.

What differentiates the Key Spot Mobile App from other mobile apps, is the ability users have to create and control their own advertisements within the app. As I developed the Key Spot Mobile App, I thought about people who travel and how they would find local gems, activities, and restaurants within the city they were visiting.

Having decades of experience in the technology industry, this was the right time for me to make my impact. In 2016 I developed the affordable Key Spot mobile application platform that can be used by everyone for sharing and finding out what is happening in the community. The mission for my IT Company Quality SAP is to provide affordable mobile application services and products and give back to the community. Developing this platform aligned with my mission. With the launch of the Key Spot Mobile application platform, it was a way to offer small businesses the opportunity to save on mobile application development cost while being able to share their business and services with the community.

The Key Spot Mobile App was developed to be used by a broad audience, who is looking to find and share positive events, activities, and services, with their community. The mobile app has great features for sharing with friends, and other reporting functionality.

Cynthia McCalister, owner of Quality SAP and founder of the Key Spot App

Affordability

With the Key Spot Mobile App platform, users can create an advertisement for as little as $24.99 for a one week ad. This package includes features that allow business owners to promote deals as well as, creating and tracking coupons. Now, small business owners can share their special offerings without spending an arm and a leg.

Features

Just about everyone has a mobile device. The Key Spot Mobile App enables users with this product to stay informed and find hidden gems. It's great for travelers, since it uses GPS technology. It also provides alerts and notifications, offers sharing features, reporting, and more to makes the Key Spot Mobile App platform, useful.

More than Just Technology

The mission of Quality SAP is to supports small businesses. With an ad on the Key Spot app, a business becomes part of the Key Spot Business Partner Network. We support our mission by helping to spread the word about each business and service, that is part of the Key Spot Business Partners Network. In addition, we promote networking among the partners to help grow business relationships and future opportunities.

Statistics:

- About three-quarters of U.S. adults (77%) say they own a smartphone. **(Pewresearch)**

- The smartphone is becoming an important tool for shoppers. Pewresearch.com, used for many shopping decisions. **(Pewresearch)**

- Many people rely on smartphones to access the internet. **(Pewresearch)**

- In the US 90 percent of consumer's mobile time is spent in apps. **(Yahoo Flurry analytics)**

- Mobile and tablet usage surpassed desktops last year. Mobile and tablet usage was 51.3% while that of the desktop was 48.7%. **(StatCounter)**

- 80% of the internet users around the globe have a smartphone. **(Smart Insights)**

- Of all the internet traffic, 56% comes from mobile devices. **(SimilarWeb)**

- The population of mobile users has been increasing at the steady rate of 12.6% per year. **(eMarketer)**

- At this pace, it's expected that the number of smartphone users across the globe would surpass 2 billion by the end of 2016. **(eMarketer)**

- 51.7% of the world's population will have a smartphone by 2018. **(eMarketer)**

- Mobile advertising is expected to represent 72% of all US digital ad spending. **(Payfirma)**

- It is expected that the number of mobile friendly retailers will grow by roughly 300% in the coming years. **(Luxury Daily)**

- 78% of mobile searches for local business information result in a purchase. **(Kissmetrics)**

- Over 47% of small businesses are likely to have a mobile application by 2018. **(Kissmetrics)**

- 56% of participants report visiting a brick-and-mortar store after receiving a deal or offer on their mobile device when they were near the store. (**PRRI-US**)

Chapter 4 Tips: Effective Ways to Use the Key Spot Mobile App Platform

- Users on the app can locate places to visit and activities to do even when traveling.

- Alerts can be set to be notified about specific categories.

- The app enables users to affordably share deals, discounts, services and events within the community using mobile technology.

- Key Spot offers a self-service functionality, which allows the user to manage and control their advertisement.

- Reports allow for tracking purchases and sales, based on the Key Spot Mobile App advertisement offers.

- Key Spot has an easy to share feature, which allows you to spread the word about your advertisement to your network.

- More than just technology, it's a network working to support small businesses and connect small business owners with other Key Spot Business Partners

5 PRINT MEDIA CAMPAIGNS: PAPER PLEASE

"The way to get started is to quit talking and begin doing."
Walt Disney

Print media is considered printed material for marketing, such as newspapers, post cards, and magazine ads. To make the most impact for your business utilizing print media, consider creating a marketing campaign. Don't stop at having an ad in your local newspaper and or magazine. Think about updating your business cards and creating a business postcard in order to support your marketing campaign.

Examples of Postcard Marketing for the Key Spot Mobile App

The key to print media is to have the specific message clearly articulated on your material. There have been many ad campaigns we have utilized to market the Key Spot app. During the holidays, we focused on what was important to the consumer, which was finding deals and getting savings. One of the marketing campaigns we did was create post cards showing deals and discounts available on the app along with information about what the Key Spot app has to offer. One side of the post card promoted the mobile app, the other side promoted business savings found on the app.

During the summer, people are looking forward to vacation and going to events like festivals and concerts to have fun. Along with businesses, the Key Spot app is also used for promoting Artists and Performers, by sharing their upcoming events. We were fortunate to work with a local band, "Zack Attack", who was marketing their concerts on the Key Spot app. We created special post cards to market their band showing the band's upcoming events along with information about the Key Spot app. We would have Key Spot representatives attend their concerts and hand out post cards and candy to the attendees. Attending the events offered a great opportunity to reach potential customers.

Key Spot Band Promotion for Zack Attack during Out Door Concert, July 2016.

Suggestions for Promoting your Business and Brand

Postcards are great for giving high-level information in order to get people interested in learning more about your business or event. Find local events and opportunities, in order to share information. Sometimes, receiving printed materials face-to-face is more effective, than just a mailer. That way, those who receive a postcard can ask questions instead of just throwing a mailer away. When handing out postcards, I would walked door-to-door and meet business owners. This was my opportunity to share information about specific events and benefits of the Key Spot Mobile App.

If you are looking to provide more detail about your business, one great tool to use is a brochure. A brochure allows you to give more context about your mission statement, the purpose of your business, the products and services you provide, and how you will benefit the user. Lastly, creating a brochure allows those on the receiving end's questions to be answered. In your brochure, provide contact information on how people can reach you. Showcase upcoming events or promotions to get the audience to take action. Don't be too wordy, make your language clear. Have visuals to keep your readers interested. These things, along with an eye catching opening page, will help make your communication better for those looking to understand more about your product or service.

Get in the habit of always having your business cards on hand. Creating a business card can be beneficial in order to network with other industry professionals, and to gain business from new consumers. A business card is your friend. You can provide all the contact information needed for people to reach out or learn more about your business. Include in your card a catchy slogan that is used for your business. Provide key information such as the following to allow people to contact you and lead them to finding more information about your business.

Key business card Information

- Your name
- Your company's name
- Phone number
- E-mail address
- Website
- Services and or products offered
- Any social media sites

Tips on Printing Materials for Your Business

Have a visually appealing layout for your marketing material. Be sure the reader's eyes are drawn to the important aspects of the messaging. When you are almost ready for print, do a final proofread of your items for any grammar errors, etc. before printing any of your business materials. Having multiple grammar errors on any printed materials for your business will appear to be unprofessional. Once that is completed, you will be ready to have your materials professionally printed.

When I first started my business I was given a wake-up call. Someone I shared my business information with gave me real talk. They said, "Your presentation and products are great, but you must do better with your printed materials."

I cannot stress the importance of spending extra money to make your printed material look as professional and classy as possible. In the end, it could make the difference between gaining customers by looking serious about your business, or coming across as an amateur.

Additional Ways to Utilize Print Media

There are several other ways that you can utilize print media, even if you're not physically handing it out to potential consumers.

- Mail printed materials out to a targeted audience or location
- Utilize event bags
- Find opportunities where vendors are needed and share your marketing materials, examples: expos, business functions, or organization events.

Lastly, having family and friends that support your business can be beneficial. You can give them your printed materials, in order to share with others within their network. Print media is still being utilized to share information. It remains a great way to spread the word about your business or service.

Statistics:

- The average response rate for physical mail is 4.4% while the rate for email is just 0.12%. Besides, 79% of consumers have a positive and immediate reaction on a brand's direct mail. On the other hand, the merge between printed and digital advertisements has proven to be the best solution for marketing purposes. **(b2cprint)**

- 70% of Americans prefer to read on paper and 67% prefer printed materials over digital. **(b2cprint)**

- In general, 80% of traditional mail is opened while 80% of emails is disregarded (just 20% is read). Other surveys showed that the opening rate for prospecting physical mail is 91% against 11% for advertising emails. **(b2cprint)**

- When it comes to response and lead, print advertisements also have the best figures. The average response rate for physical mail is 4.4% while the rate for email is just 0.12%. **(b2cprint)**

- The merge between printed and digital advertisements has proven to be the best solution for marketing purposes. **(b2cprint)**

- Those online marketing campaigns that include printed catalogs produce 163% more profits than those campaigns that only use digital media. **(b2cprint)**

- According to Forbes Magazine, print materials and publications offer your customers and prospects a brand experience that can't be replicated online. **(b2cprint)**

Chapter 5 Tips: Ways to be Successful with Print Media

- Create a print media campaign strategy.

- Find creative ways to share your printed materials.

- Utilize event bags to market your business.

- Before printing, have someone proofread your materials.

- Be sure that your materials are professionally printed.

- Use a combination of print media such as, business cards, post cards, and brochures.

- Share your printed materials face-to-face with others.

- Always include your company logo on your printed materials and website.

- Be sure to include a QR code that will direct users to your website or other marketing site.

6 MAKE A VIDEO: LIGHTS, CAMERA, ACTION

"When everything seems to be going against you, remember that the airplane takes off against the wind, not with it."
Henry Ford

Videos are the one thing that is most often shared amongst users on social media. No matter if it's the latest video of a well-known singer, a funny commercial, or a video that captures a prank, these are the types of videos, that oftentimes go viral overnight. One viral video can give a person millions of views, which can launch your brand instantaneously.

Successful Ways to Create a Video

In order to make a successful video for your company, begin with a concept. What is the key message you want to get across to others? Think about how you will communicate your topic, in a short video. Be sure to make a video that will stand out amongst your competition, by being amusing, entertaining, or informational. Lastly, in order to keep the interest of your viewers, remember to keep your video less than two minutes long.

Tools for Creating a Video

There are many tools available in order for you to create a short video. If you don't know where to begin, you can always start by checking out tutorials on creating short videos on YouTube.

In order to maintain consistency, be sure to create a production schedule. You may even want to create a YouTube Channel for your business. Doing so can lead you to millions of subscribers and the possibility for you to earn advertising dollars.

One of my concepts for a video was a cheesy and fun commercial, with a catchy theme song for my product. I first wrote a script, came up with a jingle, built a set, included actors and directed, as well as produced the video. Whatever you decide, have a vision, a plan, and be sure to carry it out until the end.

Once your video is created, upload it to YouTube. Use keywords with hashtags, which will make it easy for users to find it. You can also share the link to your video via email and text message, with family, friends, clients, and followers. Just remember to be creative, use the resources you have, and put you vision out there. You never know, your video just might go viral.

Statistics:

- More than 500 million hours of videos are watched on YouTube each day. **(Bufferapp)**

- 87% of online marketers use video content. **(Outbrain)**

- 45% of people watch more than an hour of Facebook or YouTube videos a week. **(Wordstream)**

- 85% of the US internet audience watches videos online. **(Chiptompson)**

- The 25-34 (millennial) age group watches the most online videos and men spend 40% more time watching videos on the internet than women. **(Wordstream)**

- 92 percent of mobile video viewers share videos with others. **(Virtuets)**

- 51% of marketing professionals worldwide name video as the type of content with the best ROI. **(Insivia)**

- Marketers who use video grow revenue 49% faster than non-video users. **(Wordstream)**

- Videos up to 2 minutes long get the most engagement. **(Insivia)**

- Native videos on Facebook have 10 times higher reach compared to YouTube links. **(Socialbakers)**

- Viewers retain 95% of a message when they watch it in a video compared to 10% when reading it in text. **(Insivia)**

- Videos about product features are most popular, followed by how-tos and professional reviews. **(Thinkwithgoogle)**

- In 2016, video content was responsible for 69% of all the internet traffic. **(Smart Insights)**

- People like to spend time watching videos on Facebook and YouTube. Noticeably, 19% of the users like to spend 4 or more hours watching YouTube videos, compared to only 10% of Facebook videos. **(Smart Insights)**

Chapter 6 Tips: Marketing tips for you Video

- Begin with a message of what you want to get across to your viewers.

- Make your video funny, catchy, entertaining, and informational.

- Create a production schedule.

- Make your video less than two minutes long.

- Create your own channel on platforms such as YouTube.

- Launch your videos, in order to align with specific events.

- Share the link to your video with family, friends, clients and followers via e-mail and text message.

- Use keywords and hashtags in order for others to find it.

7 NETWORKING: NO WORK WITHOUT NETWORK

"Work hard, be kind, and amazing things will happen."

Conan O'Brien

Networking is defined as, "the exchange of information or services among individuals, groups or institutions; specifically for the cultivation of productive relationships for employment or business." (merriam-webster.com). As a business owner, you should always have a networking mindset. You never know whom you'll meet and the opportunities that will come your way. You have to learn to be a go getter and open to going out into the world by yourself. You may be in a room where there is absolutely no one that you know. But go in with a positive attitude, a smile, and look friendly and approachable.

I try to attend as many networking events as possible. The more events you attend, the more possibilities are available to you. Before each event, I prepare myself by having my business cards and postcards available for potential clients.

Advice on Networking

- Be mindful that some people you network with may not be interested in your product or service at the time

- Be prepared by having brief talking points

- Always remain passionate

- Consistency is key

- Always keep track of the people whom you encounter

- Keep up with any business cards that you may receive

- Remember to follow-up with potential clients, via e-mail or phone call, and schedule meetings

No is not bad

Not every business networking encounter goes the way you want. Think of a "no" as a "not right now", but maybe next time around. After a while of meeting people, and sharing your services and business, you may feel like your efforts are in vein. Don't get defeated. One great way to stay positive as you work the room and share your passion, is to think about how the next person you meet might be your big break. Having persistence is necessary in order to be successful.

There have been times when I attended different events and saw the same people over again. The first go round, I present my business offer and get a maybe. Next event, I catch up and reunite with the same people again, giving another opportunity to share updates and present my business offer. By then, they are more familiar with me and may have more questions. When the 3rd and 4th time comes around, and I run into the same individuals, they are pretty versed with what I have to offer. The difference is, they may introduce me to someone who has not heard of my business, or decide they are ready to try it out. That persistence can lead to a door open or at least cracked, to share an offer to someone else who might be more interested. So, you never know what each day has to offer. Stay positive no matter what, and be persistent.

With that in mind, have your brief talking points always at the ready. Be prepared to briefly describe your product and services. Give common examples of how it can be used, or what it is that you are marketing. Having visuals is always helpful.

In large group settings, you may see people talking together in clusters all around the room. Don't be afraid to go up to strangers and listen into the discussion. When you get an opening, introduce yourself and share something interesting to the group.

As you are making your rounds introducing yourself to people, though you are eager to share what you do and what you are all about, don't forget to hear what others have to say. Be open to meeting different people, building relationships, and learning something new. You might not come out with a sale, but you can come out with a new opportunity in the future, a referral, a mentor, or building a new friendship. The more networking you do, the better you get at networking.

After you have completed your networking and gathered your contact information, don't forget the most important thing, you must follow up! Send emails the next day to say thank you or show interest in talking more. If too much time goes by, the moment is lost. Once you do get a response, be sure to schedule a meeting to reconnect and work toward closing a deal. In reality, you may end up sending more than one communication before you receive a response. I advise at least 3 follow up emails a few weeks apart, before you choose to give up. On average, it takes at least 6 touch points before a sale is made.

Outside of networking events, other great ways to meet people in business or potential customers is by attending festivals, fairs, expos, where people have vendor tables. In some cases these can be free events to attend. It is a great opportunity to share your information with business owners at tables. They are a captive audience. Go up and introduce yourself. Learn about their product or services, then share your information and how you can benefit or help them as well. Leave your card and visual handouts so they have a take away from you, following the event. Don't forget to follow up.

In the end, networking doesn't stop. Remember, it is not a one and done activity. There are a lot of follow ups and repetition involved. Think of each day as an opportunity. Always be ready to pitch your product, because today just might be the day for your big breakthrough.

Statistics

- It Takes 6 to 8 Touches to Generate a Viable Sales Lead. **(Salesforce)**

- The average person deletes 48% of the emails they receive every day. This task takes them just five minutes. **(Mashable)**

- The vast majority of prospects want to read emails at 5 and 6 a.m. To send messages early use email tools to schedule them. **(Hubspot)**

- The most effective words to put in your email subject line: **(Mashable)**

    - Demo
    - Connect
    - Cancellation
    - Apply
    - Opportunity
    - Conference
    - Payments

- The most ineffective words to use in your email subject line are: **Mashable**

- o Assistance
- o Speaker
- o Press
- o Social
- o Invite
- o Join
- o Confirm

- An all caps subject line hurts response rates by approximately 30%. **(Boomerang)**

- Subject lines with three to four words get more responses than shorter and longer ones. **(Boomerang)**

- The Boomerang team also found messages written at a third-grade reading level are 36% more likely to get a reply than those written at the college reading level. **(Boomerang)**

- The more you write, the less likely you are to get a response. Only one in three messages that are longer than 2500 words receive a reply. However, you shouldn't be too brief: A 25-word email is roughly as effective as a 2000-word one. What's the sweet spot? Between 50 and 125 words -- or around the length of this paragraph. **(Boomerang)**

- Don't just provide information -- request some, too. Emails that contain one to three questions are 50% likelier to get replies than emails without any questions. **(Boomerang)**

- 95% say that in-person meetings are essential for any long-term business relationship. **(Forbes.com)**

Chapter 7 Tips: Expand Your Network & Grow Your Brand

- Join business organizations and chambers.

- Take part in business expos, festivals, and fairs.

- Network at different events.

- Be sure to follow-up with people whom you meet.

- It takes at least 6 touch points before a sale is made.

- Ways in which your touch points can work are by, sending e-mails, making phone calls, connecting on LinkedIn, handing out business and post cards, and interacting with potential clients via social media.

- Attend a networking event, at least twice a month.

- Always have your business cards, post cards, and fliers handy.

- Be sure to get contact information for potential clients.

- To help you remember who you have spoken to at a networking event, be sure to keep their business card and make note of it.

- Know your elevator pitch, in case you have an opportunity to speak with an investor.

- Be approachable and a go-getter.

- Remember to state your name clearly when introducing yourself.

- As you speak, be sure to repeat the person's name with whom you are conversing with.

- Find connections as you network such as, common interests and people you both may know.

- Always end a conversation with a "thank you" or, "it was great speaking with you today".

- Be sure to schedule a follow-up meeting with those who have shown interest in your product, service, or brand.

8 EMAIL MARKETING CAMPAIGN: SEND IT NOW

"You are what you think. So just think big, believe big, act big, work big, give big, forgive big, laugh big, love big, and live big."

Andrew Carnegie

Email marketing is defined as "the use of email to develop relationships with potential customers or clients. Email marketing is one segment of Internet marketing, which encompasses online marketing via websites social media blogs, etc. It is essentially the same as direct mail except, instead of sending mail through the postal service, messages are sent via email." (Ward, 2017)

Email marketing is either hit or miss. Oftentimes, you may not receive a response from the people you send your marketing campaigns to. This is because people are quick to delete or disregard an email they deem to be not of importance. Or, sometimes your emails could be sent to several other places, such as junk mail or marked as spam.

According to buildfire.com, there are several tools available to assist you in supporting your email marketing campaigns. Examples include, Litmus, Reachmail, Mailchimp, and Targethero just to name a few. Cool thing is, most of these tools offer a 7-day free trial! (Blair, 2017)

Though sending out emails in bulk to multiple recipients may seem like a time saver and support a higher probability of gaining profits, due to the numbers game, there are still times when a personal email can be just as effective. When sending out personal emails to recipients, you should make your message more specific. When you are wording your message, tie in details about the recipient. This will help the communication come across as more genuine. When a person feels a connection, they are more likely to want to learn more about the product or service being offered.

Personal Emails

When sending personal emails, there are several key things you must take into consideration. According to mindtools.com, you should, "make good use of subject lines." Having a good subject line, will not only catch your reader's attention but, they will more-than-likely not disregard your email.

Secondly, be sure to "keep your messages clear and brief. The body of an email should be direct and informative, and it should contain all pertinent information." (mindtools.com). Lastly, be sure to proofread any and all emails before hitting send! There is nothing worse than sending an email about your business, with multiple grammar errors.

Tips for Sending Personal Email Messages

- Open your email with a personal greeting

- Provide background information about how you met and where you met your recipient

- Briefly mention how the recipient can benefit from your product, service, and brand

- Propose dates and times for a follow up meeting to learn more about them and share how your product/service can be of benefit to them

- Be sure to close your email with "looking forward to hearing from you" and "Thank you in advance"

After Sending a Personal Email

- Track your email message

- Send a follow-up message if you do not receive a response, 1-2 weeks after your initial email.

- If no response is received after the following-up, be sure to send another email one month later.

I have sent out tens of thousands of emails, using several different approaches. Those email communications have led to building new business relationships, brand recognition, and an increase in application users.

Whether you choose multiple recipient email marketing campaigns or sending personal emails, the best option may depend on your purpose.

When you are building out an email marketing campaign, there are several different approaches for getting your email marketing campaign across. One way is by choosing to create a periodic newsletter, sharing the latest specials or activities related to your business. Use an email as an opportunity to promote seasonal specials. For instance, create a fall sale for back to school offers, or coupons for the Christmas season. The purpose of your email should drive recipients to your website and to make a purchase. In order to make this possible, action and urgency must be included in order for this approach to be effective. Be sure any communication sent out via email is interesting and creative. You want people to be drawn into what you have to share.

Lastly, once communication is sent via email, be sure to keep tabs on your statistics. Many of the tools for sending mass email messages, include tracking features, which allow you to see your email message open rate. You can also manage your data using a tracking sheet. The more you communicate and track your responses, the more effective your email marketing campaign will be.

Statistics:

- Automated email messages average 70.5% higher open rates and 152% higher click-through rates than "business as usual" marketing messages **(Epsilon Email Institute)**

- Personalized email messages improve click-through rates by an average of 14% and conversions by 10% **(Aberdeen)**

- 74% of marketers say targeted personalization increases customer engagement **(eConsultancy)**

- Emails with personalized subject lines are 26% more likely to be opened **(Campaign Monitor)**

- Personalized emails deliver six times higher transaction rates **(Experian)**

- 53% of marketers say "ongoing, personalized communication with existing customers results in moderate to significant revenue impact" **(DemandGen)**

- Personalized promotional emails had 29% higher unique open rates and 41% more unique click-through rates in 2013 **(Experian)**

- Email is 40 times more effective at acquiring new customers than Facebook or Twitter **(McKinsey)**

- When it comes to purchases made as a result of receiving a marketing message, email has the highest conversion rate when compared to social, direct mail and more

- Email subscribers are 3 times more likely to share your content via social media than visitors from other sources. **(QuickSprout)**

- Email marketing drives more conversions than any other marketing channel, including search and social. **(Monetate)**

- Sending four emails in a month instead of one significantly increases the number of consumers opening more than one email **(Whoishostingthis)**

- The average order value of an email is at least three times higher than that of social media **(McKinsey)**

- Email's ROI was 28.5% compared to 7% for direct mail **(Cheifmarketer)**

- For every $1 spent, email marketing generates $38 in ROI **(CampaignMonitor)**

- 90% of email's get delivered to the intended recipient's inbox **(CampaignMonitor)**

- 68% of Americans say they base their decision to open an email on the "from name" **(CampaignMonitior)**

- 83% of B2B marketers, use email newsletters for content marketing **(Content Marketing Institute)**

- Open rate is highest when companies send two emails per month **(Database Marketing Institute)**

- Email remains the channel most buyers employ to share content with 94% saying the email was their number one channel for sharing **(DemandGen Report – 2017 ContentPreferences Survey)**

- The average person deletes 48% of the emails they receive every day and can take up to five minutes **(Mashable)**

- The vast majority of prospects want to read emails at 5-6 a.m. **(Mashable)**

- According to Mashable, the most effective words to use in an email subject line is, demo, connect, cancellation, apply, opportunity, conference, and payments **(Mashable)**

- The most ineffective words to use in an email subject line are, assistance, speaker, press, social, invite, join and confirm **(Mashable)**

- According to Boomerang's analysis of 300,000 emails, an all CAPS subject line hurts response rates by approximately 30% **(Boomerangapp)**

- Subject lines with three to four words get more responses than shorter and longer subject lines **(Bommerangapp)**

- The Boomerang team found messages written at a third grade reading level, are 36% more likely to get a reply than those written at the college reading level **(Boomerangapp)**

- The more you write in an email, the less likely you are to get a response **(Boomerangapp)**

- Only one in three messages that are longer than 2500 words receive a reply message **(Boomerangapp)**

- A 25-word email is roughly as effective as a 2000 word email **(Boomerangapp)**

- The sweet spot for an email message is between 50-125 words **(Boomerangapp)**

- Emails that contain between one to three questions, are 50% more-than-likely to get replies, than email messages without questions **(Boomerangapp)**

- An email campaign is six times more likely to get a click-through as compared to a tweet **(Business 2 Community)**

- In 2016, personalized email messages received an 18.8% open rate, while those without personalization received a 13.1% open rate **(Business 2 Community)**

Chapter 8 Tips: Enhancing Your Email Marketing Approach

- Make sure you have a good subject line.

- In the body of your email, share how your readers can benefit from your services.

- Keep your messages clear and brief.

- Track your responses.

- In a mass marketing email, send email messages on a bi-weekly or monthly basis and on special occasions.

- Utilize built-in tools to track the open rate of your email messages.

9 WRITTEN PUBLICATION: PUT IT IN WRITING

"The most difficult thing is the decision to act, the rest is merely tenacity."
Amelia Earhart

In this chapter, we will focus on affordable ways to utilize written publications, to help support your business marketing.

There is usually a built-in audience with larger publications, which gives you the opportunity to reach people who you may not have the opportunity otherwise to connect with.

Ways to Get Your Brand Noticed by the Public

- Contribute your knowledge, by sharing in the comments section in key publications

- Create a press release

- Create your own blog and be sure to post at least once a week

- Contact journalists who specialize in writing articles about people in the community

Share Your Comments

You will see more and more how references from comments people post on twitter, Instagram, Facebook or other sources are included in news commentaries, talk show commentaries, and news articles. What you write can end up being seen by are larger audience, if you have the right spotlight on your material.

Publish a Press Release

You can make a big splash with a press release. This is an opportunity to have a feature written all about you. You can show your journey, your area of expertise, your focus for your business, and how you want to provide your service to others. In my experience I have had success with media Press Release articles written about my business and area of expertise. Utilizing a professional service to have an article written about you is a way to get your information out to the public. One company that specializes in Press Releases which spotlight people in the community is "Making Headline News", a company started by Andre Johnson. It provides features for business owners and others impacting the community. They share their story with the public, and it is also provided to news outlets who may be interested in further exploring the story. When I utilized the service, I had tens of thousands of readers of my article, which provided further exposure to my business.

Become a Blogger

If you decide you want to be in control of your publishing, then try starting your own blog. A blog is a great way for you to have your own media. Have people come to you and see what information you have to share. I like the idea of bringing people to me instead of always having to reach out to find people who want my business. Though in reality, you are always building your network and reaching out to others, this is one channel where they may choose to find you. My expertise is sharing the stories of small business owners and words of wisdom they have to offer. I create a weekly blog dedicated to small business owners and their stories. They share how they got started and what they learned along the way. Find a niche and begin exploring the world of blogging. Be sure to include a variety of topics generating interest and new readers. Build a following and begin getting your brand out there for others to see.

Partner with Journalists

Another option is to identify journalists who specialize in writing articles about people in the community, your business category, or service reviews of your industry. Reach out to them and share your business. There may be an opportunity to contribute to their news story, or they can choose to do a write up specifically about your business. With their established audience, any mention of your name and business will provide instant exposure that will benefit your brand.

There is power in written publications. People like to read, whether online or in the newspaper. Go forward and leverage this vehicle to your advantage. Start your own blog, put out a press release, or leverage existing media outlets to share your brand.

Statistics:

- 53% of marketers say blog content creation is their top inbound marketing priority. **(Hubspot)**

- 1 in 10 blog posts is compounding, meaning organic search increases their traffic over time. **(Hubspot)**

- In many markets, white papers and case studies continue to be effective. **(Forbes)**

- Content marketing leaders experience 7.8 times more site traffic than non-leaders. **(Contentmarketinginstitute)**

- 56% of marketers believe that personalized content promotes higher engagement rates. **(2015 IBM Digital Experience Survey)**

- The top three things that make content effective: audience relevance (58 percent); engaging and compelling storytelling (57 percent); triggers a response/action (54 percent). **(LinkedIn Technology Marketing Community)**

- Prescriptive content that lays out a formula for success was the most popular type of content among B2B buyers in 2017, with 97 percent citing it. **(DemandGen Report – 2017 Content Preferences Survey)**

- Top three content marketing objectives: Drive sales and/or leads; engage customers/buyers/influencers; boost brand awareness. **(Curata)**

- Eighty seven percent of B2B buyers give more credence to industry influencer content. **(DemandGen Report – 2017 Content Preferences Survey)**

Chapter 9 Tips: Practices for Effective Written Communication

- Identify publications where you can contribute topics.

- Utilize media outlets to get your brand noticed.

- Consistently provide comments on articles posted on social media.

- Write reviews that you have experience with and share how they benefit your brand.

- Create a press release.

- Create a blog and post daily or weekly.

- Contact local journalists that specialize in writing custom features for people in the community and business articles.

10 HOST AN EVENT: PRESENTED BY YOU

"The future belongs to those who believe in the beauty of their dreams."

Eleanor Roosevelt

Hosting your own event is a great option to expose others to your brand and expand it. It also gives you the capability to control who you want your audience to be, the focus of the event, and what you want others to gain.

Organizing an event can be a huge ordeal. Here are several questions to consider.

- What type of event do you want to host?
- Who is your target audience?

- What is the timeframe for organizing your event?
- Do you have a team to assist with executing this event successfully?
- What is your budget for the event?
- How will you be marketing your event?

These are all crucial questions that will help determine what direction you will want to go. There is a lot of work put into organizing an event, so don't just go at it alone. Have a team to help you put it together and support you. Sometimes multiple heads are better than one. You can also choose to combine forces and make it a joint event with another partnering sponsor. This allows you to multiply the audience by including your network, your partner's network, and bringing in other interested parties to the event. As the leader of the event and organizer, you hold the cards to bringing in your target audience, marketing the event in the way you like, and learning from each event you host. The more people begin to know about you, the more likely your brand will be top of mind to others. Soon, you will begin to get calls and emails from people asking, "When is your next event?".

Depending on your budget and objective, there are multiple approaches you can take for organizing your event. You can choose to do a free and open to the public activity, or a paid activity. With a free event, you may have more attendance. If there is a cost associated with the event for attendees, though the participation might be less, you have more opportunity to generate income. It's all up to what you want your desired outcome to be. Be sure you share your event often, and in advanced on social media. Post it on platforms such as Eventbrite, which will allow other potential parties to find out about the event and register.

My Experience

With my company Quality SAP, we have always been advocates for connecting communities. Our mission is to support small businesses and give back to the community. One way we have done this is by hosting events open to the public. One of the best ways that has worked for us when hosting an event, is to find a partner and make it a joint effort. Partnering up is a win in many ways. As a business, you are always looking to get exposure. When you partner with another organization, you both benefit from bringing in people from different markets to your event. Though partnerships are great, it is important to first establish roles for each partner. For example, you may have a partner who owns a large facility for hosting the event. The way you can contribute is by organizing and marketing the event. Both parties will reach out and share the event with their respective contacts and clients. From there, look forward to a great event.

I am a fan of community organizations like the YMCA or local Community Centers, and enjoy supporting the youth. Putting on events to provide positive activities for teenagers has been a joy for me. In addition, for our events we include a charitable contribution to local non-profit organizations, donating portions of the proceeds. Giving back is always a good idea. When you decide to organize an event, it may be helpful to include a charitable aspect. I have hosted over a hundred events in my professional career. There can be lessons learned from each event. Some really great and rewarding events I've hosted were youth focused events. One example is when my company partnered with one of the largest YMCA's in the area to organize a Dance Competition. We had so much support from business professionals, organizations, the local TV media, and young talent across the area who came to perform and showcase their skills. It was a big success. The event was an example of how working with other organizations can lead to a successful event, while also helping to provide brand exposure in the community. This is a great model I have used for large events. When you are going big, it's better to team up with another business or organization than to go it alone.

The Ralph J. Srolle Countryside YMCA Leader's Club And Pure Silk Photographic Creations Present The Next Level

Bring It!
Cincinnati-Dayton Regional Teen Dance Competition

Collaboration between Pure Silk Photographic Creations and Countryside YMCA to Organize Teen Dance Competition Event, May 2009.

Hosting events specific to business networking is another great way to connect with business owners, if that is your goal. I have also had success working with other business owners to co-sponsor business networking events. One example was an event where I partnered with another Key Spot Business Partner, Full Throttle Indoor Karting. Full Throttle was the event host and my company was the organizer. We called it the Small Business Networking Event, and added a twist, with a go kart racing competition. The event was a great example of how businesses can come together to partner and share in promotion.

Partnership between Full Throttle and Key Spot app to organize Small Business Networking Event, April 2017.

In order to make any even a success, you have to take the time to market it effectively and spread the word to get people excited. When promoting on social media, do initial posts at least 2 months in advanced. As the event gets closer, do weekly, then daily communications. Use tools like print media to give post cards out to people you know, and hand out to others you meet as you begin to network and socialize the event. For my events, I would hit the pavement and go door to door to different businesses, talking to people and inviting them to attend. Hand out thousands of printed material in order to get the attendance level you are looking to reach. Send out email blasts to your business distribution list. Use your local radio to promote your event. Don't forget to share with your networking resources such as your Chambers and Business Organizations. They are more likely to provide support for you because of your association with the organization.

Television advertising commercials can be very expensive. There are other ways you can promote your event on TV to the public, without spending the tens of thousands of dollars on a commercial. Start by identifying news stations that have segments where they spotlight positive people, events, or other local activity in the community. Send an email and follow up with a phone call to the news station about your event. Make it a point to be persistent and reach out to multiple outlets. Once you get that "Yes", that is your opportunity to shine bright and bring your cause to the public. If you are the sponsor, this is your opportunity to share the importance of the cause and how your business supports positivity. When you do good and support the community, people tend to want to support businesses like yours. This exposure now brings awareness to others about the work you are doing in the community, and recognizing your brand as one to watch.

If you are not wanting to host an event, there are always opportunities to be part of someone else's event as a vendor. Just remember, as a vendor the focus is not solely on you and your message. The benefit of being a vendor is introducing your services to those who visit your table, along with networking with other vendors that are part of the event.

Overall, hosting an event is a great way to get your name known. Whether people attend or not, having received your information via email, printed material, social media, or word of mouth, you are building brand recognition. That's what we call a win!

Statistics

- The typical cost of hiring a full service event planner accounts for 15-20% of the total event budget. **(Cost Helper)**

- Social media is the most effective way to spread the word about an in-person event. **(Marketing Charts)**

- 71% of all ticket purchases are made online. **(Bizzabo)**

- On average, 46% of total event revenue comes from registration/ticket sales. **(Planning Pod)**

- The top three most popular event management software products are: Eventbrite, Cvent, and Eventzilla. **(Capterra)**

- 74% of product or service users become regular customers after an "experiential" marketing event. **(EventTrack)**

Chapter 10 Tips: Market Your Business with an Event

- If you are looking to attract a kid friendly audience, try hosting a fun activity at a local park, kid friendly venue, or partner with a school.

- Look for opportunities to advance common positive causes like health, self-esteem, sharing talent, or incorporate a learning activity.

- If you are looking to focus your event on groups such as high school or college students, include activities that may be interesting for them where they can work in teams, participate in giving back to the community, or take part in a competition.

- When it comes to business professionals, some great suggestions that draw a crowd are happy hours, business expos, seminars, and workshops.

- Establish a team to execute your event.

- Have a plan and objective for your event.

- Partner when possible, especially for large events.

- Give back to a good cause.

- Make your event informational, interactive, and fun.

- Market your event in advance and often, weekly then daily leading up to the event.

- Use tools like Eventbrite to provide ticketing services for your event.

11 BUILD YOUR OWN FRANCHISE OR AFFILIATE: FRANCHISE YOU

"Twenty years from now, you will be more disappointed by the things that you didn't do than by the ones you did do, so throw off the bowlines, sail away from safe harbor, catch the trade winds in your sails. Explore, Dream, Discover."

Mark Twain

As I was thinking about ways to grow my business, one thing that came to mind is that, I can't be the only one talking about it. I need to build a network of people across the country who are sharing my product with others. That's when I decided to start my own affiliate network or franchise. I call them my Key Spot Growth Partners. If you think in terms of restaurants like McDonalds, the first restaurant was started in San Bernardino, California. What would have happened if they chose never to franchise? People around the country and the world would not be familiar with the brand. Instead, they made the decision to start their first franchise in Des Plaines, IL, and the rest is history.

If you want to grow, then do it. Think big and grow big. Today you will find my Key Spot mobile app being used around the nation, from Seattle to New York. I have Key Spot Growth Partners all across the country helping to spread the word about how people can use the mobile app to affordably share their business, services, and events with the community.

When you share your passion and vision with people, you will be surprised by how many "Yes's" you get. The first thing you must do is believe in yourself and what you have to offer, before you are ready to share with anyone else. Start off with your pitch and proposal for franchising. It takes a lot a practice and iterations to put together the right package to present your business proposal. Start by outlining background information about your business. Include information such as who you are, why you want to partner, and what's in it for them. Present the information in a format that is easy to understand. Reach out to potential partners to share your idea. It may take several discussions before an agreement is made. With any partnership, be sure to have a formal contract in place. Keep track of progress and communicate on a routine cadence.

There are so many benefits you get from partnering with others to be affiliates or franchises for your business. Since there is financial gain for them, they are excited to help you expand. The benefit for you is having the opportunity to grow in areas you might have never reached on your own. This partnership helps accelerate your brand name across different areas. Another benefit from expanding your brand recognition is the additional capital received from people who choose to enlist your product or service.

If you have not thought of this option, then consider how you can take your business, and package it in a way which would allow others to help sell it for you. Make it a win-win for all. Start by believing in yourself, and sharing your message with others who also believe in you. There's nothing to it but to do it! I have done it and you can too.

Example of affiliates for the Key Spot mobile app.

Statistics:

- It is estimated that the franchise industry accounts for approximately 50% of all retail sales in the US. **(azfranchises)**

- Most franchise companies have fewer than 100 units. **(azfranchises)**

- Top franchise company- McDonalds. **(azfranchises)**

- Success rates for franchises are greater than 90%, making this the lowest failure rate of any type of business. **(Entrepreneur Magazine)**

- There are More than 300 different industries and business categories that use the franchising business model as a means to distribute goods and services. **(azfranchises)**

Chapter 11 Tips: Franchising You

- In order to grow and expand your brand, you can't do it all by yourself. Rely on others to help through affiliate partnerships and franchising.

- Build your network and make relationships that can become potential partnership opportunities for growth.

- For your affiliate package proposal, create a template and payment structure that can be leveraged along with providing incentive to those looking to get on board.

- Have the same messaging tools to share the information with other potential partners.

- Think big, and share your business across the country.

- It takes time to expand, so be diligent and stay patient knowing your hard work will pay off in the long run.

12 ALWAYS A LESSON TO BE LEARNED: MAKE LEMONS INTO LEMONADE

"There are no secrets to success. It is the result of preparation, hard work, and learning from failure."

Colin Powell.

As part of the road to success, there will always be learning opportunities that come your way. You can't learn and grow without going through failures. Think of a failure as a positive, it's like a course corrector. This is your opportunity to step back and re-evaluate your course, then make adjustments as needed. It took Thomas Edison 1,000 tries to successfully create the light bulb. When he was asked, how it felt to fail 1,000 times, his response was "I didn't fail 1,000 times. The light bulb was an invention with 1,000 steps."

After taking the tips provided from this book, and going off to try new approaches, there may be some areas where you don't get the instant success you are looking for. There is not a one size fits all approach, or magic pill that will instantly make you rich and successful. It truly is all about you, your work ethic, and your attitude. If you put in the work and persevere long enough, you will win.

Along with the many wins, I also have had learning opportunities that have come my way. Sometimes your vision doesn't always work out as planned. Here is one example of a great learning opportunity. I had an idea about putting on a great event that would bring together communities across the city and surrounding areas. I called it the SPARK Olympics. SPARK stood for Supporting Physical Activity and Recreation for Kids. My goal was to get families out of the house and their neighborhood silos, and have a fun Olympic style competition of neighbors and families. A lot of effort went into planning, marketing, sponsorship, and trying to spread the word about the event. There was marketing done through television, radio, flyers, Word of Mouth, and social media.

The intention was good, having a positive outdoor event to bring families together, but there were a few factors that impacted the success. Because it was a first time event, there was a big unknown about turn out. The idea of a cross community event was a new concept to many people, so it was harder to get the support. Then, the biggest factor was the timing. The idea was to have a fun outdoor event, but it was scheduled for the beginning of spring. The day leading up to the event, the weather forecast was snow and cold. Since the weather was in the 50s and 60s a few days prior, that wasn't a concern because it seemed unlikely to really snow. The weather predictions were only accurate 50% of the time. I had planned to have the event take place rain or shine. But then, waking up the day of the event, there was actually snow on the ground. As I started checking emails, I saw people sending cancelation messages. Soon I began getting calls, again about people cancelling their attendance. We pressed on to set up for the event and continued to execute. There ended up being only a few people willing to brave the cold and come out to support the event, not nearly what I was hoping for. It was definitely not the expected outcome, based on all of the hard work that was put into planning the event. As they say, "When life gives you lemons, make lemonade". I tried to take that experience and learn from it. My key take a ways were lessons that would help me with planning even bigger and better events.

Some positives that did come out of the experience

- More exposure in the community about my company and positive activity we were doing.

- We were able to identify additional partners for future events.
- We also were able to contribute to a worthy non-profit organization.

Though every attempt may not always be a winner, there is always something positive to gain to make it better next time around.

Chapter 12 Tips: Make Lemons into Lemonade

- Keep your head up and stay positive. There is always next time.

- Regroup your team and do a retrospective to capture lessons learned.

- Identify any wins that still resulted from your efforts.

- Identify improvements on what you can change for the future.

- Turn to your support system and leverage their wisdom to help you through your journey.

13 WHO ARE YOUR MOTIVATORS: MOTIVATING MAVENS

"If you want to lift yourself up, lift up someone else."

Booker T. Washington

Who are your motivators? These are the people in your life that will help and inspire you along the way. They are not just cheerleaders, but they are active participants in helping you reach your vision. As a business owner, you can't just go at it alone. You have to have special people in your life that will help you along the way. They will be there for you in the highs and lows of your journey. For me, there have been many motivators in various stages along my path. Each one has been a value to me, and the success that I have become as a person and with my business.

Jeni, the Next Level Motivator. I was introduced to Jeni while working an event at one of the largest YMCA's in the country. She was the event director and leader of the youth programs at the YMCA. When I began the Next Level Program, focused on bringing youth together and sharing positive experiences, we partnered to make that vision a reality. She was a big supporter of the program. Having the support of people like Jeni and the YMCA organization helped us reach many youth and provide great programming and fellowship opportunities. One of the great events we organized was the Teen Dance Competition. With the Next Level Program, teens were able to build relationships and take part in activities that they normally would not have, leaving many great memories to last them a lifetime.

Christina, the Big Picture Motivator. Christina was a great motivator encouraging the growth of the photograph workstream of my business. She was always providing her support, and looking for opportunities to provide photography services for events. She played a big role in the increase of events Pure Silk was able to participate in and exposure that was received. She was an advocate to others about the company and a great sales person. Her commitment to seeing the business succeed was appreciated and valued.

Rhoda, the Fountain of Knowledge Motivator. Rhoda possessed a wealth of knowledge and experience. She was the gem that helped provide guidance during the early stages of starting the mobile app workstream of my business. She spent many years providing consulting for women business owners. She had been the president of the Women's Chamber of Commerce and held many workshops and training sessions. Rhoda was a guiding light for me and a mentor, providing not only inspiration but instruction. She would share what to do and what not to do, review information and help me prepare for key presentations to ensure my success. I am so thankful for her service and guidance. She has helped me get to where I am today with my professionalism, when it comes to presentations and being able to lead workshops.

Mandisa, the Dream Motivator. Think big and do big things! Having such a special friend for so many years, we have supported each other throughout our ups and downs. One thing that has always stayed consistent is the support we have of each other to pursue our Dreams. When I look to someone to share the latest venture going on in my life, she is one that I go to. We both follow the motto think big and do big things, because "I Can Do All Things through Christ Who Strengthens Me" (Philippians 4:13).

Paula, the Diamond Motivator. We had known each other for many years. We were both members of the same diversity organization, which is where we met. Through life's journey we were separated, but one day after leaving the Big Lots Shopping store, on my way out to the car, I ran into Paula. After sharing a warm embrace and briefly catching up with each other, in passing I mention my work to develop my mobile application that will help connect communities and support small businesses. I was so please to see and hear her excitement about my venture. When she said she was onboard to be part of the journey, I immediately added her to the team. In Paula's role as Director of Business Development, her gift for building relationships has helped spread the word about the Key Spot app. Paula's eye for detail, event organizing, and business outreach enabled me to improve my approach with marketing my business, and learn from each event that was organized. She would always say, "Be sure you have your spiel", which means, have your talking points ready at all times. You never know when the next "yes" will come. I truly appreciate her influence with helping me to be a better communicator.

Denise, the Social Media Marketing Motivator. It was Denise that helped expose me to social media, and provided the yes you can attitude when creative ideas came to mind to market and promote my business. Denise came in my life through our kids. She also happened to be my neighbor. Her background was marketing and social media with large companies. She was a great add to the team, helping to start our business journey into the world of social media. She introduced me to Facebook, Mailchimp, and shared her social media savvy to help start my company on the road to success building our network. We organized many events, and even included local personalities in our ventures. I am so thankful to have built my relationship with Denise and learned from her the skills of using social media to help market my business and reach others.

Stevie, the Business Networking Motivator. Stevie is what I call a true advocate. An advocate is defined as "a person who publicly supports or recommends a particular cause or policy." Stevie has been an advocate for me and my business. She started an organization called Cincinnati Women's Collaborative Network (CinCWN), which is a resource group for women in business. Her mission has been to see women business owners win and be successful. Stevie has given me opportunities to partner with her organization with the Key Spot app. She has also publically shared and communicated my services with others. I have called or texted her with ideas and suggestions, and she has always provided her honest advice. Her wisdom has been a value to me. One of the great lessons she shared with me was "Know your worth. You can't give everything you have for free. You have a great service to offer and people will compensate you for your products." Her advice continues to motivate me, knowing that my mission is not in vein.

Kate, Quyen, and Sherry, these ladies are what I call my Rock Star Motivators. As a mother, naturally I meet new friends via kid's sports. From being on the same soccer team, these wonderful women have grown to become my close friends and supporters. Besides watching the kids play sports, the moms have lots to talk about. I would often share my activities and what new ideas I had for my business. They were always there to encourage me, help spread the word about my Key Spot app, in fact Sherry was one of the first people to download the Key Spot app. Over the years, Kate and Quyen supported me as models for marketing promotions. All three have starred in videos for Key Spot. I am so thankful to have these Rock Star Motivators in my life. They are always willing to support me in whatever way they can.

Monica and Angeline, the Girl Power Motivators. I call them that because they would always say how strong I am and proud of the work I have done for my business while balancing a family. They would make efforts to connect me to other influencers to help spread the word about my business, and attend functions, and events I organized to support me. Trying to make a business work on your own will leave you broke and by yourself. Having people in your life who can share your passion, and open doors with the right connections can help you get to the next level. That is what you call a support system. *Brian Tracy, Entrepreneur and Author* stated,

"Successful people are always looking for opportunities to help others. Unsuccessful people are asking, what's in it for me?". When you have people in your life who can help you, always remember to help others as well along the way.

Mary and Roslyn, what I call my Mom Motivators. Before my mother passed away, she was always my biggest cheerleader. She supported every venture I pursued and gave me the pep talks, prayer, and push I needed to stay motivated to pursue my path. Mary and Roslyn, my aunts, have been my Mom Motivators to help keep me going and ensure my mother's spirit and encouragement lived on through them. Whether it was introducing opportunities for me to share my business, investing in my dream, praying me through tough times, or giving guidance, my aunts have been there to motivate me and keep me strong through the rough patches and cheer me on during the good times.

Shannetta, my Master Motivator. She has been with me all of my life, being my sister. She has always given me support, advice, and guidance when I needed it. If it wasn't for her, I would not be where I am today as a business owner. She has been a true supporting vessel of knowledge. Every idea and suggestion I have had to help support my business ventures, she has heard and provided her thoughts and feedback. Sometimes every idea is not the best, but when there are gems, she will encourage me and do everything she can to support me. Whether it is attending events, investing money and resources, sharing information with others, reviewing information, she has been there. I am truly blessed to have such a wonderful and loving sister that has been my cheerleader and motivator throughout my life.

14 WORDS OF WISDOM: FROM KEY SPOT BUSINESS PARTNERS

"Our greatest weakness lies in giving up. The most certain way to succeed is always to try just one more time."

Thomas Edison.

My company, Quality SAP, truly values and supports the small business owners who utilize our Key Spot app and business network. We call them, Key Spot Business Partners. Each week we celebrate a business owner by sharing their journey and words of wisdom to help other small business owners. These words are driven from their passion, experience, and lessons they have learned along the way. Here are some words of wisdom which may help provide encouragement and enlightenment for you as well, as you go through your journey.

Alton James, Ph.D., President of JIV Media
(www.jivmedia.com) - Mount Clemens, MI

> "Study the work of other professionals out there. Be the best you can technically, but always develop your own style and voice. Beyond that, it is important to network and create a team of trusted people you can rely on for aspects of your business. Lastly, always put yourself in a position to learn and showcase your abilities to a wider audience; focus on what makes you unique and success will follow!"

Joe O'Gorman Co-Owner of Full Throttle Indoor Karting
(www.gofullthrottle.com) – Cincinnati, OH

> "Stay resilient and optimistic. You will hear lots of "no's" Keep looking for the "yeses"! It took them three attempts to find financing, and they looked at over 30 properties before they found the right one with a landlord that was willing to lease to a startup, and a city that was supportive of small business. Be ready to adapt the plan to overcome the obstacles, or to move forward."

Leatriece Franklin, Owner of LF Mobile Life Saving Courses (www.lfmobilelifesaving.com) - Memphis, TN

"Never quit, and remember why you went into business in the first place. The reason can vary for many but money making should not be the sole motivator. At times exhaustion will set in, you feel alone, you may not make the money that you envisioned or you may not get the customers/clients that you want. It is at those times that you dig in and keep pushing. Remember, it may be a slow process getting to where you dream, but you will get there with patience, drive, and determination. A slow start with a quality product means more to her than anything."

Vic & Jill Malone, Co-Owners of IMPACT Fitness Training (www.Impactfitnesstraining.net) – West Chester, OH

"A great and successful organization must surround itself with great people and must provide equally great service. The second is, avoid using financing to capitalize your company-- and then only as a last resort. "

Mike Stokes, Owner of Cincy Brew Bus Tours (www.cincybrewbus.com) – Cincinnati, OH

"Before you go into business for yourself, make sure you check all of the regulations surrounding the business. Be prepared to work incredibly hard, and for long hours. Manage your expenses carefully. Finally, remember that you will make mistakes along the way."

Stevie Swain, Owner of Swain Consulting LLC (www.swainconsultingllc.com) – Cincinnati, OH

"Utilize the path set for you in life to find your true God given gifts. She never would have thought she'd be in business for herself, but through the path set before her she is now able to serve others with education gained from previous employment paths. Another great piece of advice is to always stay focused!"

Bonita Carlisle, CEO/President of Bonita's Southern Style Sweet Potato Pies – Cincinnati, OH

"Never give up on your dreams and visions. Be sure to surround yourself with like-minded people and organizations who can help guide you down the right path. Finally, remember that "God will make room for your gifts." Proverbs 18:16 KJV."

Dan McCalister, CPT and Owner of Dan Fitness LLC (www.danfitness4u.com) – Cincinnati, OH

"Run your business, don't let your business run you. When starting off, you take on everything and don't have any regard for your time. As you grow, don't let time control you. Have a plan and continue to make goals. As you achieve one goal, set another. Don't stop growing in your profession. Constantly learn and don't stop learning."

Mrs. Jimmie Walker, Owner of Family Concepts (www.familyconcepts.org) – Cincinnati, OH

"While money is important, it should not be the primary motivation for the work you do. Whether it is a non-profit or for profit business, serving and helping others should be the focus."

Gail Lee Gardner, Founder of She Was Made LLC (www.shewasmade.com) - Cincinnati, OH

"When you have a calling in your life to do something, surrender and be obedient. Everything happens for a reason. Even if you don't succeed, there is a lesson you can take away and learn from your experience. There is no such thing as a failure. It is the challenges that force you to take inventory, evaluate your situation, make adjustments, try new things, and get back on the right path. Put in the work, then let things happen organically. When you let things go, then your blessings begin to flow."

Rosemary Oglesby-Henry, CEO of Rosemary's Babies Co. (www.rosemarysbabies.co) – Cincinnati, OH

"When they go low, it's not enough to go high, THAT'S WHEN YOU FLY. Failure to launch in business or in life is not an option. Sometimes you have to go around a wall rather than through it. Though life is not easy, no one can beat you down lower than you, but no one can lift you up higher than you. And finally, after all is said and done, legacy is how you live and what you leave behind."

Ciara Jordan, Owner of Made With Love Cakes & Catering Services – Dayton, OH

"Even when it is tough and hard, don't quit. Sometimes when challenges come, and times get tough you have to pick yourself up and continue on your journey. Don't forget that you chose your path for a reason. Trust yourself, follow your goals, and see it through."

Whitney Barkley, Owner of Speakerazzi (www.speakerazzi.com) – Columbus, OH

"If you are working to build your brand by blogging, realize it is a marathon not a sprint. Focus on having good content, motivate, and provide tips. Work with other business owners to cross promote, you share and they share, so you all can lift each other up."

Shannetta Dewberry, Owner of Crown Jewel Designs (www.crownjeweldesigns.com) – Dayton, OH

"When God puts a passion in your heart, pursue that passion. Never give up and never stop. If it is something that comes to you, then it is God sent. You owe it to yourself to continue to pursue it. Don't let negativity interfere with what God has put in your heart, because it is there for a reason.

Have fortitude and tenacity and you will achieve your dreams."

Michael Brown–Real Estate Developer, Investor, & Realtor – Dayton, OH

"Stick and stay with your dream. If it is a passion of yours, make it happen. If you are looking to be a great success financially, nurture your big dreams and ideas, and turn them into your full time endeavor."

Marc & Aaron Johnson, Co-Owners of Neighborhood Ice Cream Truck (www.neighborhoodicecreamtruck.com) – Dallas, TX

"Be flexible. Realize that sometimes you have to change your business model. The consumers will guide you to where you need to go. They started out driving ice cream trucks, now they are doing kiosks, deliveries, & wholesale. Another piece of advice is to objectively assess your business. Identify what works and what doesn't, then make changes where needed. Be persistent and don't give up on your dream. And finally, know your God and be prayerful. Many times they felt like they would have to shut their doors, but because of faith, they were able to make a way."

Amy Elberfeld, Owner of Styling with Amy (www.stylingwithamy.com) – Cincinnati, OH

Show people that you love not only your product but what you do! Set up procedures for business, including a plan for follow-up with potential and current clients. Find networking groups that you enjoy and offer opportunities to connect with new people."

Mindy Galloway, Owner of Bag VOYAAGE (www.bagvoyaage.com) – Detroit, MI

" Taken from the bible "Write the vision, and make it plain" Habakkuk 2:2 (KJV). Have a solid plan, and keep it in front of you. A lot of times people come up with a great idea. They write it down, but then they fold it up and leave it somewhere to collect dust. Keep after your ideas. Also, do not be afraid to fail. In every failure, there is a growth and learning opportunity. Finally, don't give up on your dream."

April Ferguson, Owner of APRO Accounting & Tax Services LLC (www.aproaccounting.com) – Cincinnati, OH

"When you are starting a new business sometimes you don't know what you don't know. It is better to spend money today to get the guidance you need, which can help you save hundreds or thousands down the road. When it comes to finances, people set up businesses without knowing what they need, then end up owing money in the end. Having a finance professional to help you on your journey can make your path a lot easier. Finally, be prepared when tax season comes around. Start organizing your financial information at the end of the year."

Brenda Ellison Program Director of Face 2 Face Radio Talk Show on KLAY (www.agomoregon.com) - Lakewood, WA

"Nothing that we do in life is left to chance. Believe everything is set for your life. Take possession of your life, and not just your business."

Darrin Brown, Founder of Dynamic Leadership Empowerment Group (www.dynamicleadership.expert) - Houston, TX

"Operate your business only in your areas of gifts and talents. If you do that, then it will fulfill you even during hard times. Otherwise, if it is not your passion, you will get mediocre results. Motivation is temporary, but inspiration comes from within. Only inspiration is sustainable. If you are living your passion then the ups and downs don't stop you. Also, invest in yourself, and build a foundation structure to be successful. Finally, be sure to spend your time with like-minded and mission-minded individuals who will help you achieve your vision."

Sean & Dawn Bradford, Owners of Grind24 (www.grind24.net) - Satellite Beach, FL

"Never quit, no matter what. Things are going to be up and down. That is the nature of being your own boss and having your own business. Also, you have to continually work on yourself. In order to be the person you want to be and deal with people and the public, you have to work on your personal development. It is easy to get frustrated and discouraged. If you don't hear the positive voice in your head and how you feel about you then you can't be 100 percent. Remember the 80/20/100 Rule, 80% nutrition, 20% fitness, 100% positive mindset. Having a positive mindset helps you have all the pieces together."

Leslie Williams, Founder of Survivors on Purpose (www.survivorsonpurpose.com) – Arlington, TX

> "Be sure the work you do is coming from the right place, and from the heart. Have passion for the work you are doing. Always be humble and have a servant's heart. Be aware, there are personal sacrifices."

Antroinette Worsham, Founder of T1 Diabetes Journey (www.t1diabetesjourney.org) – Cincinnati, OH

> "Take something personal and run with it by making it your passion. No matter what, never give up. Trust in God and his plan for you. Finally, remember to keep moving forward. As Dr. Martin Luther King Jr. once said, "If you can't fly then run, if you can't run then walk, if you can't walk then crawl, but whatever you do you have to keep moving forward." "

15 CLOSING

"You miss 100 percent of the shots you don't take."

Wayne Gretzky

Now that you know there are plenty of options for you to try, which will allow you to reach out and share your brand, it is up to you to determine what approach you want to begin with. These are all great ways that have helped me, and I hope you can apply them as well to help move your business to the next level. Each option may provide a boost in a different way. The key is trying new things. For me, I always had hope that the right person would see my video, hear me on the radio, read my story, see my product and be moved by my mission. Keep your hope alive, don't let up on your dream, and you will reach your goal. Put together your plan, and determine what your financial opportunities are to invest in utilizing different marketing techniques. Then, just get started. There's nothing to it but to do it! Don't be afraid to make mistakes along the way. Hey, at least you can say, I tried that! Be bold, and go big! Don't forget, YES YOU CAN!

Statistics:

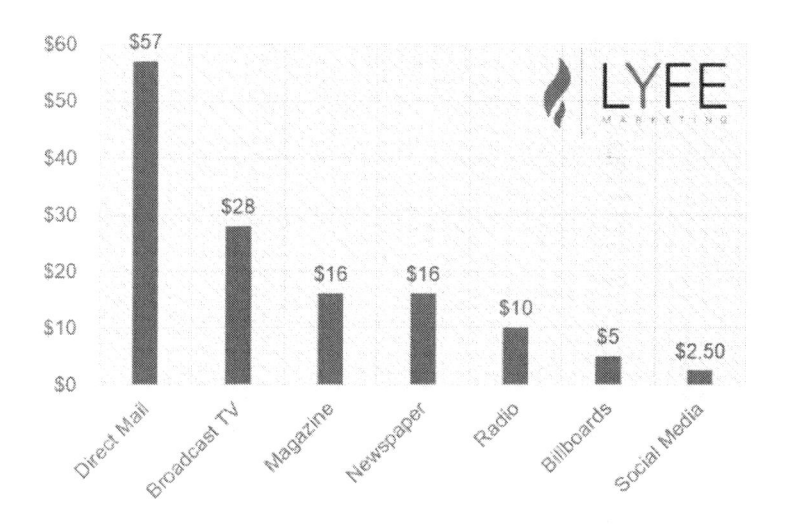

Cost Comparisons statistics. Cost to reach 1,000 users or impressions. **lyfemarketing**

Next Steps:

Having the information to know what options you have and understanding the time and cost involved, will help you determine your investment path for your business. Keep your passion going and follow these next steps to guide you on your road to success.

- Identify your goal.

- Build your roadmap to success.

- Leverage the lessons and guidance provided to try new tools and approaches to make your success happen.

- Identify your motivators and keep them close.

- Build your network.

- Take risks and go for it!

ABOUT THE AUTHOR

Cynthia McCalister is an Ohio Native. She has been a leader in Information Technology for over 20 years, working at top fortune 100 companies. She holds a Master of Science Degree in Information Technology Management from Colorado Technical University, a Bachelor of Science Degree in Electrical Engineering from Wright State University, and a wealth of Certifications including: Project Management Professional (PMP), Certified Scrum Master (CSM), SAFe Program Consultant (SPC) and more.

Cynthia McCalister, MS

Cynthia started the IT Company Quality SAP in 2007, which stands for Quality, Service, and Products. The mission, inspired by her parents Thomas (who was a small business owner) and Madlyn (who worked for non-profit organizations within the community) is to Support Small Businesses and give back to the Community. It is a Certified Minority & Female Owned Business. Quality SAP offers affordable mobile technology platforms, such as the Key Spot mobile app, used by business owners across the country to share information within the community. Also under the umbrella of Quality SAP is Pure Silk Photographic Creations, a Photography company specializing in Green Screen Technology, and Quality SAP's training and application development division.

She is also the Founder of the SPARK Olympics, which stands for Supporting Physical Activity and Recreation for Kids. It is a family event bringing communities together and promoting fun competition, physical activity, and recreation. As well as Co-Author of the book, "Open Your Gifts Book 2".

With decades of experience in business marketing techniques and tools, Cynthia offers a wealth of knowledge to share with others. Cynthia's motivation is her husband and children. She continuously strives to demonstrate that "Anything is possible to achieve with God, a Dream, and Hard Work".

WANT TO LEARN MORE

Learn more: Visit www.keyspotapp.com or www.qualitysap.com

Download the Key Spot mobile App: Visit www.keyspotapp.com

For any of the following or other inquiries, email cjmccalister@qualitysap.com:

- Scheduling a Business Marketing Workshop in Your Area
- Meet the Author Book Signings
- Speaking Engagements
- SPARK Olympics Events in Your Community
- Interview bookings
- Networking Opportunities
- Becoming a Key Spot Business Partner
- Key Spot Growth Partnerships
- Technology Training
- Learning more about the Key Spot app for your business or organization

Connect on Social Media:

- **Facebook:** www.facebook.com/KeySpotApp
- **Facebook Group:** www.facebook.com/groups/KeySpotBusinessPartners
- **Twitter:** www.twitter.com/KeySpotApp
- **Instagram:** www.instagram.com/keyspotapp
- **LinkedIn:** www.linkedin.com/in/qualitysap

NOTES:

Radio:

- www.statista.com/topics/1330/radio/
- www.edisonresearch.com/hacking-commuter-code-really-happens-commuters-driving/
- www.nielsen.com/us/en/insights/news/2017/tops-of-2017-audio.html
- www.strategicmediainc.com

Social Media

- https://www.statista.com/statistics/246230/share-of-us-internet-users-who-use-selected-social-networks/
- https://devrix.com/tutorial/small-business-marketing-statistics-trends-2018/
- https://digital.com/blog/small-business-statistics/#ixzz566RtFWF1
- http://www.curata.com/blog/content-marketing-statistics-the-ultimate-list/
- http://mashable.com/2012/02/09/boomerang-email-infographic/#tiJF183wYqqP
- http://gs.statcounter.com/press/mobile-and-tablet-internet-usage-exceeds-desktop-for-first-time-worldwide
- http://www.smartinsights.com/mobile-marketing/mobile-marketing-analytics/mobile-marketing-statistics/
-

Mobile

- http://www.similarweb.com/corp/resources/the-state-of-mobile-web-in-the-us-2015/
- https://www.emarketer.com/Article/2-Billion-Consumers-Worldwide-Smartphones-by-2016/1011694
- https://www.payfirma.com/blog/50-mobile-facts-and-stats-every-merchant-needs-to-know/
- http://www.luxurydaily.com/real-time-retail-will-revolutionize-retailing-as-we-know-it-report/

Email

- https://www.campaignmonitor.com/blog/email-marketing/2016/01/70-email-marketing-stats-you-need-to-know/
- https://blog.kissmetrics.com/surprising-mobile-ecommerce/
- http://prrius.org/spotlight/2017-email-marketing-retail-study/
- http://www.emailinstitute.com/premium/q4-2012-north-american-email-trends-and-benchmarks
- http://www.aberdeen.com/research/7635/ra-social-media-marketing/content.aspx
- https://econsultancy.com/reports/the-realities-of-online-personalisation-report
- http://press.experian.com/United-States/Press-Release/experian-marketing-services-study-finds-personalized-emails-generate-six.aspx
- https://blog.demandmetric.com/wp-content/uploads/2014/09/Customer-Marketing-Benchmark-Report.pdf

- http://www.experian.com/marketing-services/email-marketing-quarterly-benchmark-study-q2-2013.html?WT.srch=PR_EMS_Q213Benchmark_082813_press

- https://www.campaignmonitor.com/resources/guides/email-marketing-new-rules/

- https://thedma.org/blog/data-driven-marketing/saturday-stat-series/

- https://www.quicksprout.com/2013/04/04/11-things-i-wish-i-knew-before-i-started-my-first-blog/

- http://www.monetate.com/

- http://www.emailmonday.com/dma-national-client-email-report-2015

- http://www.whoishostingthis.com/blog/2014/02/12/email-deliverability-101/

- https://blog.bufferapp.com/social-media-video-marketing-statistics

- http://www.outbrain.com/blog/state-of-content-marketing-2012

- https://www.wordstream.com/blog/ws/2017/03/08/video-marketing-statistics

- http://chipthompson.com/19-fascinating-statistics-case-visual-content-marketing/

- https://www.virtuets.com/45-video-marketing-statistics/

- http://www.insivia.com/27-video-stats-2017/

- https://wistia.com/blog/optimal-video-length

- https://www.socialbakers.com/blog/1452-facebook-videos-have-a-10x-higher-viral-reach-than-youtube-links
- http://www.insivia.com/50-must-know-stats-about-video-marketing-2016/
- https://www.thinkwithgoogle.com/consumer-insights/the-changing-face-b2b-marketing/
- http://mashable.com/2012/02/09/boomerang-email-infographic/#tiJF183wYqqP
- http://blog.boomerangapp.com/2017/05/the-one-thing-you-should-never-do-in-an-email-subject-based-on-data/
- http://www.business2community.com/marketing/50-statistics-latest-marketing-trends-strategies-2017-01865218#zF4Ic82vYdhsFYpJ.97
- http://www.emailmonday.com/dma-national-client-email-report-2015

Print Media

- https://www.b2cprint.com/what-statistics-say-about-printed-advertisements-effectiveness/

Video:

- https://www.statista.com/statistics/274050/quarterly-numbers-of-linkedin-members/
- https://www.statista.com/statistics/272014/global-social-networks-ranked-by-number-of-users/
- https://www.omnicoreagency.com/linkedin-statistics/
- http://blog.linkedin.com/2014/04/18/the-next-three-billion/

- http://get.simplymeasured.com/rs/simplymeasured/images/InstagramStudy2014Q3.pdf?mkt_tok=3RkMMJWWfF9wsRolua%2FAZKXonjHpfsX56%2BgtXaC0lMI%2F0ER3fOvrPUfGjI4CTsViI%2BSLDwEYGJlv6SgFQrDEMal41bgNWRM%3D
- https://oursocialtimes.com/16-statistics-to-show-why-marketers-need-instagram/
- http://www.business2community.com/marketing/20-fascinating-statistics-marketing-2014-infographic-0711604#WffwIZbPVz52yfOz.99%20
- http://www.business2community.com/marketing/20-fascinating-statistics-marketing-2014-infographic-0711604#WffwIZbPVz52yfOz.99%20
- http://danzarrella.com/infographic-how-to-get-more-likes-comments-and-shares-on-facebook.html
- http://contentmarketinginstitute.com/wp-content/uploads/2015/09/2016_B2B_Report_Final.pdf
- http://www.smartinsights.com/content-management/content-marketing-strategy/content-marketing-europe-2016/

Networking:

- https://www.salesforce.com/blog/2015/04/takes-6-8-touches-generate-viable-sales-lead-heres-why-gp.html
- **https://blog.hubspot.com/sales/sales-statistics**
- http://mashable.com/2012/02/09/boomerang-email-infographic/#tiJF183wYqqP
- http://blog.boomerangapp.com/2017/05/the-one-thing-you-should-never-do-in-an-email-subject-based-on-data/

- http://blog.boomerangapp.com/2016/02/7-tips-for-getting-more-responses-to-your-emails-with-data/
- **www.Forbes.com**

Email Marketing:

- http://www.emailinstitute.com/premium/q4-2012-north-american-email-trends-and-benchmarks
- http://www.aberdeen.com/research/7635/ra-social-media-marketing/content.aspx
- https://econsultancy.com/reports/the-realities-of-online-personalisation-report
- https://www.campaignmonitor.com/resources/guides/email-marketing-new-rules/
- http://press.experian.com/United-States/Press-Release/experian-marketing-services-study-finds-personalized-emails-generate-six.aspx
- https://blog.demandmetric.com/wp-content/uploads/2014/09/Customer-Marketing-Benchmark-Report.pdf
- http://www.experian.com/marketing-services/email-marketing-quarterly-benchmark-study-q2-2013.html?WT.srch=PR_EMS_Q213Benchmark_082813_press
- https://www.campaignmonitor.com/resources/guides/email-marketing-new-rules/
- https://thedma.org/blog/data-driven-marketing/saturday-stat-series/
- https://www.quicksprout.com/2013/04/04/11-things-i-wish-i-knew-before-i-started-my-first-blog/

- http://www.monetate.com/
- http://www.whoishostingthis.com/blog/2014/02/12/email-deliverability-101/
- http://www.emailmonday.com/dma-national-client-email-report-2015
- http://www.mckinsey.com/business-functions/marketing-and-sales/our-insights/why-marketers-should-keep-sending-you-emails
- https://www.campaignmonitor.com/resources/guides/email-marketing-new-rules/
- http://www.chiefmarketer.com/direct-mail-gets-most-response-but-email-has-highest-roi-dma/
- www.Forresterresearch.com
- https://www.campaignmonitor.com/resources/guides/high-performing-email/
- http://contentmarketinginstitute.com/wp-content/uploads/2015/09/2016_B2B_Report_Final.pdf
- http://www.dbmarketing.com/2011/10/how-does-frequency-of-e-mails-affect-open-click-and-conversion-rates/
- http://www.demandgenreport.com/resources/research/the-2017-content-preferences-survey-report
- https://www.campaignmonitor.com/resources/guides/why-email

Host an Event

- https://blog.capterra.com/10-event-management-statistics-and-facts-you-need-to-know-in-2017-and-beyond/
- http://smallbusiness.costhelper.com/event-planner.html
- http://www.marketingcharts.com/customer-centric-78404
- https://blog.bizzabo.com/five-statistics-that-point-to-the-future-of-the-events-industry

- https://blog.planningpod.com/2017/02/06/12-event-industry-statistics-that-will-make-you-think-twice-infographic/
- https://blog.capterra.com/20-popular-event-management-software-solutions-infographic/
- http://www.eventmarketer.com/wp-content/uploads/2016/05/2016EventTrackExecSummary.pdf

Franchise Your Business

- https://franchise.dwyergroup.com/leading-the-service-industry/franchising-statistics/
- http://www.azfranchises.com/quick-franchise-facts/
- http://www.entrepreneur.com/article/79492
- www.franchiseusa.net

Made in the USA
Columbia, SC
30 May 2018